Walking the L

BY TCHENKA JANE SUNDERLAND

© Jane Sunderland, all rights reserved 2004

Published 2004 by Jane Sunderland
ISBN: 0-9547086-0-1

contact information: tchenka@lineone.net

Printed by Quickprint Norwich Ltd.
Telephone: 01603 768768

*From the place where
there is nowhere else to go,
I call you.*

*From that place where,
after all the twists and turns,
there is no way forward.*

A dead-end.

The centre of the labyrinth.

*Where to be
is to be simultaneously
at an end and at a beginning.*

Come to me.

Explore my mystery.

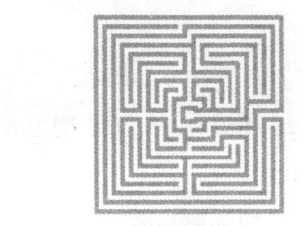

Table of Contents

What is a Labyrinth?... 1
Alpha & Omega *(meditation)*.. 4
Groundwork *(meditation)*... 6
Pattern in the Matter.. 9
Bringing into Balance *(meditation)*............................... 10
Clockwise & Anticlockwise 14
Through the Looking Glass *(meditation)*...................... 17
The Magic of Seven 20
Walking the Rainbow *(meditation)*.............................. 23
The Dynamic Dance 28
A Pilgrimage *(meditation)*.. 31
The Labyrinth & Pilgrimage 34
Contacting the Oracle *(meditation)*.............................. 38
Making Changes *(meditation)*...................................... 40

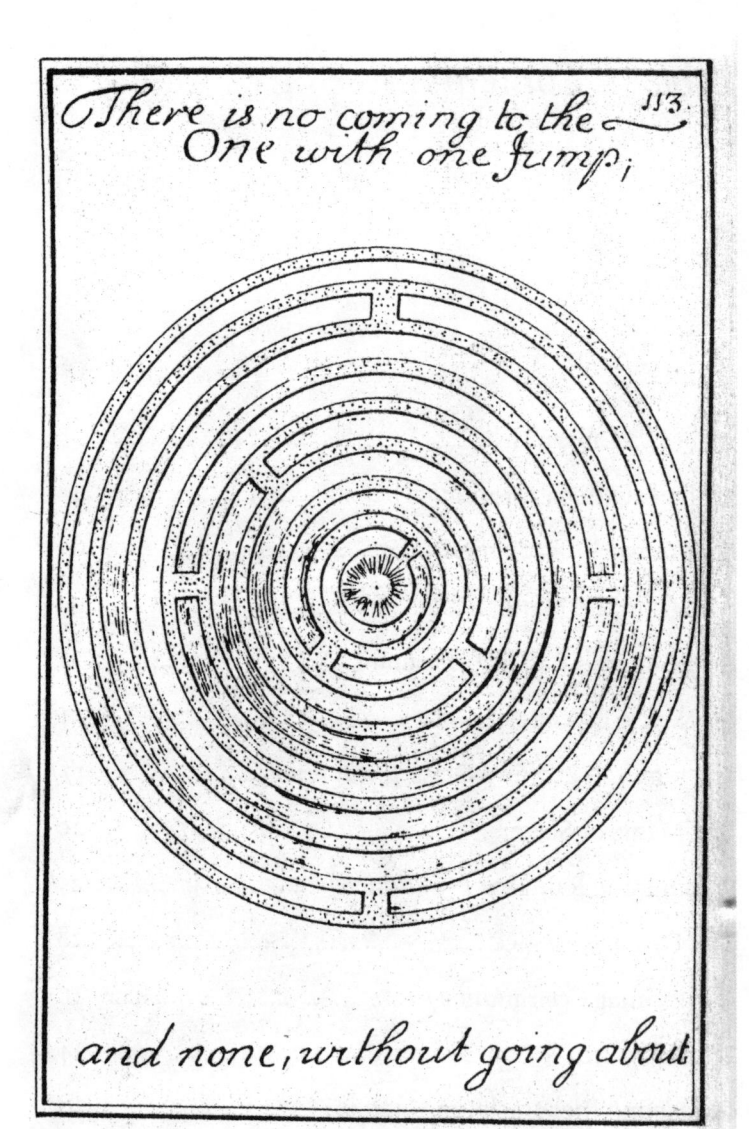

There is no coming to the
One with one jump;

and none, without going about

What is a labyrinth?

THE LABYRINTH IS NOT A MAZE. There are no choices or decisions to take. There is no way to get lost.

Whether it has seven, nine or eleven circuits, we are always lead through the larger and smaller circuits of its serpentine pathway, traversing each of its corridors once and once only, to its centre. Sometimes clockwise. Sometimes anticlockwise. Sometimes near to the centre. Sometimes far away.

Only one thing is certain. The path leads to a centre where we must stop. The only option is then to turn around and retrace our steps to the exit.

The pattern of the labyrinth is arguably one of the oldest patterns in the world. From the Americas to India, from Scandinavia to Africa we can find its mysterious coils inscribed on rock, woven into baskets, cut into the turf on village greens or laid in finest marble on cathedral floors.

No one knows where it originated but echoes of its significance resonate still in myth and folklore. Legend tells of

Theseus slaying the Minotaur who inhabited the Cretan labyrinth. Pilgrims in early Christian churches walked its pathway on their knees as a penance and pilgrimage equivalent to a trip to Jerusalem. Scandinavian fishermen ran its path before setting sail to ensure favourable winds. Midwives in southern India traced its pattern on the palms of women in childbirth in order to ease the passage of birth. It was carved on doorways to entrap mischievous spirits and prevent them entering a house. Young men are reputed to have raced to the centre to rescue young maidens during springtime fertility festivals.

The custom of circumnambulating, or walking around, a sacred centre is immemorial and cross-cultural. It is encountered in Christianity, Islam, Hinduism and indigenous belief systems. Behind all the stories it is possible to discern the underlying belief that the pathway leads to a sacred centre, back to the source, from which everything flows and from which one is reborn anew into the world.

The meaning revealed by its hidden symbolism, outlined in the following pages, leads me to believe that the labyrinth holds a key to the mystery of what can be understood as the Moving Spirit of Nature, as the vital force within matter itself that seeks to grow and evolve. Its power and purpose cannot be fully understood by the mind alone. It is a mystery that must be experienced; its pathways must be walked if their hidden power is to be released. I believe that that power is to set one on the road to becoming what, in essence, one is meant to be, to bring about an alignment between the walker and the greater forces behind the reality we inhabit.

At this time, we are experiencing a revival of interest in labyrinths. They are once again being set out as permanent features in churches and cathedrals, workshops are held during which participants walk its pattern painted on canvas floorcloths and they are laid in sand or sawdust during summer fetes and festivals.

Young and old alike feel the magnetic attraction of its pathway but there is no tradition to guide us in our approach. All too often, the cry is "what do I do?" or "what is it for?"

In the following pages I have drawn on many traditions and much personal experience to create seven exercises or forms for use in a labyrinth in order to serve different purposes or fulfil different needs. Feel free to mix and match from within the exercises so that, in time, you build your own relationship with this magical space.

May you find inspiration.

Preparation

Alpha & Omega

Alpha. Beginning

The labyrinth is a sacred space. Your experience will be enhanced if before and after each walking meditation, you prepare yourself and finish in the manner described.

With feet bare to the earth, stand still at the entrance.

1. *A touch to the forehead – think or say "as above".*
   Send your mind up into the sky as far as your imagination will carry you. Beyond the Moon. Out into the stars. See the solar system as if from outer space. Imagine hooking yourself into this spot.

2. *A touch to the abdomen – think or say "so below".*
   Bring your mind down through your body into the earth beneath your feet. Imagine roots extending down into its centre, tapping into a hidden reservoir of magnetic fire.

3. *A touch to the right shoulder – think or say " as before".*
   Project your mind to the far horizon and imagine the rest of your life stretching out before you into an unknown future.

4. A touch to the left shoulder – think or say "so behind". Send your mind back into your past and be aware of the stream of events that has brought you to this time and place.

5. Prayer-like hands pointing upwards – think or say "as without". Be aware of the four directions around you, their sounds, sights and smells.

6. Prayer-like hands pointing down – think or say "so within" Close your eyes for a moment and imagine energy from all around you flowing into your very centre.

7. Keeping your eyes closed
Imagine that you are beyond Time, Imagine that you are beyond Space Find a still, dark place deep within and rest there a moment.

Open your eyes. You are ready to begin.

Omega. Ending

When you exit the labyrinth, turn to face it. Stand still and repeat stages 1 – 4. Then

Prayer-like hands pointing down – think or say "as within"
Be aware of everything that is inside you.

Prayer-like hands pointing up – think or say "as without" whilst bringing your hands up in front of you, extending them above your head and then bringing them down in a large semi circle to either side.

It is finished.

MEDITATION ONE

Groundwork

Practise this form for walking the labyrinth as frequently as you can. Through doing so you will become comfortable within the labyrinth and will build a firm foundation for other meditations to come.

Prepare yourself to enter the labyrinth in the manner described earlier in the Alpha form.

Relax and sink your weight into the earth.
Breathe steadily, easily and deeply into the stomach.

Take one step, then another, and another.
Slowly, gently place one foot in front of another.
Feet well apart.
Weight evenly balanced.
Feel the weight shift, like sand running through an egg timer. Feel the weight shifting from one leg to another as you walk. Feel the momentum of the movement carry you forward.

Keep your awareness on your breath and in your body.
Let your eyes focus gently on the unwinding path ahead.

*Breathe easily and follow the path as gracefully as you can.
Let your arms hang at your sides – held out to the side a little for balance.*

*Take the corners as smoothly as you can.
No stops and starts. No sudden shifts and jerks.
Gracefully.
Grace – when spirit inhabits body, when heaven meets earth.*

Think of nothing, except the breath and the feel of the earth beneath your bare feet. When thoughts arise, leave them behind you on the path and focus again on the path ahead.

*Be in yourself. Be in your body. Be in your breath.
Leave your questioning, analytical mind behind.*

*Enjoy the moment.
Allow that feeling to expand.
Feel your soul begin to expand.
Feel it reach your skin.
Feel full of yourself.
Enjoy the moment.
Until you reach the centre.
The place where there is nowhere else to go.*

*Stop.
Stand still.
Motionless until the inner dynamic subsides.
Still centre within a turning world.*

Feel the body's energy settle and sink deep into the earth once more.
Be aware once more of the four directions about you, heaven above and earth beneath.

Feel your uniqueness. Hold the awareness that only you are here and now in this space and time.

Breathe deep into your body. Relax.

When the time is ripe
Turn and retrace your steps.
Through the serpentine pathways from the opposite perspective.

Dexter where it was sinister. Sinister where it was dexter.
Within becoming without. Without becoming within
Inverted and mirrored. Inside out and back to front.

Focussing on your breath. Focussing on the feel of the earth beneath your feet.

Winding up what has been unwound. Unwinding what has been wound.
Unravelling what has been woven. Weaving what has been unravelled.
Revealing what was hidden. Hiding what was revealed

When you reach the exit, perform the Omega form as outlined earlier.
Step out into the world.
Reborn

Pattern in Matter

When we walk the labyrinth our bodies move through space and time in a precise and particular pattern. Pattern is abstract, only recognised by the power of the mind whilst earth is solid matter, experienced through the sense of touch. The labyrinth is a pattern in the matter. The words matter and material are derived from the Latin *Mater*, which meant mother. The word pattern is derived from the Latin *Pater*, which meant father.

The labyrinth is a place where father meets mother. In its synthesis of pattern and matter, it celebrates a marriage of male with female, yang with yin, the above with the below, Heaven with Earth, God with Goddess. In surrendering to that pattern, you become a dancer in space and time, embodying its abstract idea, making it real in the physical world.

With practise, for after all, only practise makes perfect, there'll come a point in your labyrinthine pilgrimage when perceptions are inverted. When, quite suddenly, you are still and it is the labyrinth that is turning. Like a whirling dervish you experience for yourself the primal stillness at the core of this ever-turning world. It is at this moment that above and below, heaven and earth are as one.

MEDITATION TWO

Bringing into Balance

Through this form, you consciously draw upon the powers of the above, of Heaven, and unify them within your body with the strength and sustenance of the earth beneath your feet. Practise it frequently and in a surprisingly short time, an increased vitality and sense of wholeness will begin to develop.

Prepare yourself to enter the labyrinth in the manner described earlier in the Alpha form.

Relax and sink your weight into the earth.
Breathe steadily, easily and deeply into the stomach.

Take one step, then another, and another.
Slowly, gently place one foot in front of another.
Feet well apart.
Weight evenly balanced.
Feel the weight shift, like sand running through an egg timer. Feel the weight shifting from one leg to another as you walk.

*Feel the momentum of the movement carry you forward.
Keep your awareness on your breath and in your body.
Let your eyes focus gently on the unwinding path ahead.
Breathe easily and follow the path as gracefully as you can.
Let your arms hang at your sides – held out to the side a
little for balance.*

*Take the corners as smoothly as you can.
No stops and starts. No sudden shifts and jerks.
Gracefully.
Grace – when spirit inhabits body, when heaven meets
earth.*

*Whenever the path takes you in a clockwise direction, focus
your imagination on everything that is above you.
Mentally reach up into the sky, to the Moon, the Sun and
thence to the Stars, to everything that lies beyond. Imagine
their light and energy raining down upon you and,
emptying your mind of thought, open up to its influence.*

*Open your consciousness to the outer world. Be aware of
infinite space around you and of all possibility. Feel it
permeating every cell of your body.*

*Whenever the path takes you in an anticlockwise direction, focus your awareness on your body and on the ground
beneath you. Direct your attention to all that is inside
you. Be aware of the fluids within you. Of the tidal flux of
feeling. Be aware of gravity holding you safe, of its solidity
supporting you.*

Imagine roots stretching down from your feet to the very centre of the earth, where they tap into an enormous reservoir of molten fire. Feel its warmth through the soles of your feet.

Fire above and fire beneath.
Be conscious of the changing feelings within as your awareness switches at the labyrinth's turning points from the above to the below or from the below to the above.

When you reach the centre, be still. Close your eyes.

Imagine that the fire within the earth is rising up through your feet and as it rises, your arms slowly begin to rise at your sides. As they reach the level of your waist, you feel the energy in your abdomen. As your arms continue to rise, you feel your heart begin to warm and open and then, as your arms meet over your head, the energy enters your head where it meets the fire coming from above.

Stand still and experience the feelings within for a few moments. Imagine that you are the flame of a candle that is as big as the Earth.

Then as you allow your arms to slowly return to your sides, imagine the fires of the above travelling down through your head, your body, your legs and feet into the earth.

Revitalised, turn and begin your return journey.

As you walk the alternate clockwise and anticlockwise paths, allow your mind to focus once more on the above and the outer during clockwise circuits and on the below and inner during anticlockwise circuits. Notice that these are the opposite of what they were on your inward journey.

When you reach the exit, turn and face the labyrinth.

Perform the closing practise as outlined earlier under Omega.

Heaven and earth are united within you.

Clockwise & Anticlockwise

THE PATTERN OF THE LABYRINTH always consists of an odd number of concentric circles, commonly seven or eleven, through which the traveller moves in alternating clockwise and anticlockwise directions.

In the realms of symbolism, to move in a clockwise direction is to move with the energy of the Sun whilst to travel in an anticlockwise direction is to move with that of the Moon. We perceive the Sun rising in the east and travelling in a clockwise direction through the sky to its setting place in the west. We see the Moon travelling each night in an anticlockwise direction against its background of starry constellations.

The Sun is a star. It is the pulsing heart of the solar system, the fiery furnace of generation around which our world perpetually revolves. A year it takes to travel around the Sun. We measure our lives in terms of how many times we have travelled around it. Within the course of a year we experience a rhythmic fluctuation of light, warmth and growth, which we call spring, summer, autumn and winter. And in a lifetime we learn to recognise those seasonal cycles at work within our own lives. The Sun is an electromagnetic powerhouse, the fundamental source of all light and of all energy on earth, and therefore the source of life itself. When we travel with the Sun through the daytime sky, we move from left to right. We follow the right hand path. We follow the path of en-lightenment , of growth, of becoming, of energising, of consciousness. The Sun awakens us, energises us and sends us out into the world. We're each made to shine our own unique light. We are all made of star stuff.

The Moon reflects the light of the Sun in the darkness of the night sky, when we are asleep and the unconscious, instinctive processes of nature are in their ascendancy. It orbits the earth approximately once every 28 days and in so doing weaves an intricate and graceful tapestry with the path of the Sun, the Moon's changing shape reflecting its changing angular relationship with the Sun.

From conjunction with the Sun at New Moon, through the opposition point at Full Moon, returning to a new conjunction point at the next New Moon, the Moon waxes and wanes and in this process mediates the ebb and flow, the rhythms of life on earth, creating the months within the years. Often referred to as Stella Maris, Star of the Sea, the Moon's energy works through water, literally and metaphorically, stirring the tides, not only of the oceans but also of the deep waters of life and the unconscious. When we travel to the left, in an anticlockwise direction, we follow the left hand path. We are passive. We reflect and respond and react. We feel the tides of instinct, intuition and emotion.

Clockwise therefore symbolises the extroverted yang force. Anticlockwise symbolises the introverted yin force. Both are necessary and, just as the Sun and Moon in our sky appear to be exactly the same size, both forces are equally important. Equal and opposite. Balance between them is essential for the health and well being of the individual, the community and the natural world.

MEDITATION THREE

Through the Looking Glass

Using the labyrinth as a mirror to your Self, to your instinctive manner of behaving can be an enlightening experience.

Prepare yourself to enter the labyrinth in the manner described earlier in Alpha form.

Step forward into the labyrinth.

Relax and sink your weight into the earth.
Breathe steadily, easily and deeply into the stomach.

Take one step, then another, and another.
Slowly, gently place one foot in front of another.
Feet well apart.
Weight evenly balanced.
Feel the weight shift, like sand running through an egg timer. Feel the weight shifting from one leg to another as you walk.
Feel the momentum of the movement carry you forward.

Keep your awareness on your breath and in your body.
Let your eyes focus gently on the unwinding path ahead.

*Breathe easily and follow the path as gracefully as you can.
Let your arms hang at your sides – held out to the side a little for balance.*

*Take the corners as smoothly as you can.
No stops and starts. No sudden shifts and jerks.
Gracefully.
Grace – when spirit inhabits body, when heaven meets earth.*

*As you walk towards the centre, become aware of yourself.
Watch yourself as if from a distance.*

*Watch the tricks your mind is playing.
Be aware of those ideas that pop into your mind and distract you.
Is one topic particularly insistent or does your mind flit from one idea to another?*

*Do you surrender seriously to the process?
Do you become self-conscious and embarrassed?*

*Notice the manner in which you walk.
Do you stop and start?
Do you stumble or lose your balance?
Do you overstep the lines?
Do you rush to get to the centre?
Are you happy to trust the path or do you try to anticipate the next turn?
What is your reaction if you encounter others on the pathway?*

Are you irritated by their presence or do you welcome them as fellow travellers?
Do you give way to them readily or hold your space?
Do you smile or ignore them?

Is it hard to keep your attention focussed on the present?
Do you feel lonely?
Would you prefer company?

When you reach the centre,
Stand still and quietly reflect upon your journey
And on what you have learned about yourself.

When the time is ripe, turn and retrace your steps.

On your outward journey, imagine that you are releasing those qualities you feel are undesirable
Each time you become aware, imagine leaving them behind you on the path.

When you reach the exit, turn to face the labyrinth and repeat the Omega form as outlined earlier.

The Magic of Seven

THE CLASSICAL LABYRINTH DESIGN and that of the Norwich Cathedral labyrinth have seven circuits around their centres.

There is something very special about the number seven. When asked to choose their lucky number, most people opt for seven. God rested on the seventh day after creating the world in six. We have seven days of the week. There are seven ages of man. Life goes in seven-year cycles. Every cell in the human body is renewed in seven years. There are seven colours of the rainbow. In ancient cosmology, the seven planetary spheres encompassed the earth. There were seven pillars of wisdom. Snow white met up with seven dwarfs. There are seven deadly sins and seven chakras. Joshua marched seven times around the city of Jericho, accompanied by seven priests with seven trumpets.

What is all this about?

Mathematically it is true to say that seven is neither the product nor the factor of any other number in the decad [1 – 10] as well as being the highest number that is divisible only by itself. The geometry of seven is developed from no other system of proportion, nor does it birth any. It is impossible to draw a mathematically perfect septagon.

In the ancient science of numerology, in which numbers are imbued with meaning rather than being seen as mere computational devices, Seven is known as The Virgin number. It is connected with the functions of life, with all processes of growth and the mysteries of reproduction.

What does this mean?

A key to grasping its symbolic meaning can be gleaned from considering the seven colours of the rainbow.
Sunlight, considered throughout the world to be the purest expression of divine principles accessible by our senses, is seen as "whole" but when it is passed through a prism, or is refracted through water droplets or crystals, it splits into seven colours, red, orange, yellow, green, blue, indigo and violet. When these coloured rays are re-focussed through a prism, they magically re-combine into white light. Sunlight may therefore be perceived as "whole", but is in fact a mix of many colours, many frequencies of light overlapping. Any group of seven has therefore the hidden meaning of being the separate colours, or frequencies, that go together to make the One or Wholeness.

Consider the seven-note scale played on the white notes of the piano keyboard. Together the notes form a sequence, or pathway that leads us through distinct steps to the octave, the eighth note, which is the same note as the first but on a different level. The ancients designed musical scales both to mirror a cosmic order and to represent a model of the universe. The musical scale technically known as the diatonic scale, familiar to us in the West from time immemorial, thereby implies in its essential structure that the universe emerges from oneness, from absolute Divinity and moves through a seven stage process in order to return to absolute divinity.

So it may be in the coils of a seven-circuit labyrinth. We progress through the seven different stages or frequencies that compromise Wholeness to find on reaching the sacred centre, the eight, that place of unity wherein we are the same but different. We resonate at a new frequency. We dance to a different tune!

Meditation Four

Walking the Rainbow

There are seven colours in a rainbow, each of which is associated with one of the chakras or energy centres within the human body. Practise embodying the colours of the rainbow during a labyrinth meditation and in the process you will revitalise and balance the energies of your chakras.

Prepare yourself to enter the labyrinth in the manner described earlier in the Alpha form.

Relax and sink your weight into the earth.
Breathe steadily, easily and deeply into the stomach.
Proceeding and smoothly and gracefully as you can.

Walk your first circuit, concentrating your attention on your Solar Plexus, the location of the third chakra. Imagine there a golden yellow ball of light. It expands and becomes more luminous with every breath you take. Breathe easily and regularly. Bring the concepts of action and personal will power to mind. Hold them there and be aware of the physical sensations within your body.

As you turn into your second circuit, shift your attention down to your abdomen, the location of the second chakra. Imagine there an orange ball of light. It expands and becomes more luminous with every breath you take. Breathe easily and regularly. Bring the concepts of desire and sexuality to mind. Hold them there and be aware of the physical sensations within your body. Feel their driving power.

When you turn into your third circuit, shift your attention down again to the base your spine, to your root chakra. Imagine there a red ball of light. It expands and becomes more luminous with every breath you take. Breathe easily and regularly. Bring the concept of foundation to mind. Feel the ground beneath your feet. Be aware of gravity and weight. Feel the support of the earth and the solidity of your body.

As you turn into your fourth circuit, let your attention leap up to your heart, the location of the fourth chakra. Imagine there a green ball of light. It expands and becomes more luminous with every breath you take. Breathe easily and regularly into your chest. Bring the concept of wholeness to mind. Feel warmth radiating from your heart. Feel love and connectedness.

As you move in to make your fifth circuit, focus your awareness on a point just above the top of your head, your seventh chakra. Imagine there a violet ball of light, which becomes larger and more luminous with every breath. Imagine that this ball is itself breathing in and out. Bring the concepts of spirituality, of the immaterial realms to *mind. Try to attune yourself to their higher, more spiritual frequency. Be aware of the sensations within and around your body.*

As you turn into your sixth circuit, direct your awareness to a point between your eyebrows, your third eye or sixth chakra. Imagine there an indigo ball of light, which becomes larger and more luminous with every breath you tae. Imagine that this ball is itself breathing in and out. Bring the concepts of intuition and imagination to mind. Be aware of sensations in that part of your body and pay particular attention to sudden insights occurring on this circuit.

When you turn into your final circuit, bring your awareness down to your throat, the seat of the fifth chakra. Imagine there a beautiful blue ball of light, which becomes larger and more luminous with every breath you take. Imagine that the ball itself is breathing in an out. Bring the concepts of communication and manifestation to mind. In the beginning was the word. Be aware of accompanying sensations.

When you reach the centre, be still. Close your eyes.

Imagine that through the soles of your feet, you feel the warmth of a fire burning deep within the earth. Imagine that this fire is rising up through your feet and as it rises, your arms slowly begin to rise at your sides. As they reach the level of your waist, your feel the energy in your abdomen. As your arms continue to rise, you feel your heart begin to warm and open and then, as your arms meet over your head, the energy enters your head where it meets the fire coming from above.

Stand still and experience the feelings within for a few moments. Imagine that you are the flame of a candle that is a big as the Earth.

Then as you allow your arms to slowly return to your sides, imagine the fires of the above travelling down through your head, your body, your legs and feet into the earth.

Revitalised, turn and begin your return journey.

As you retrace your steps,
Keep your awareness on your breath and in your body.
Let your eyes focus gently on the unwinding path ahead.
Breathe easily and follow the path as gracefully as you can.

During your journey, repeat the following mantra

"My feet are on the Earth"
and consciously feel your connection with the physical realm.

"The Moon is in my abdomen".
and concentrating on that part of your body, evoke within a feeling of fluidity.

"The Sun is in my heart"
and concentrating on that part of your body, evoke within a pervasive feeling of warmth.
"The Stars are in my head" and concentrating on your head, open your imagination to images of the starry heavens.

Repeat this mantra as you walk, letting your attention move through your body with each phrase.

When you reach the exit, stop and turn to face the labyrinth.

Perform the closing practise as outlined earlier under Omega.

The Dynamic Dance

IN MYTH AND TRADITION the labyrinth has commonly been associated with a dance. Myth tells of Theseus and his companions joining arms and dancing their freedom on Delos after escaping death at the hands of the Cretan Minotaur in his labyrinthine lair. A folk dance of this Greek island, still danced today, is called the Crane Dance and is described as a circling in a pattern that closely resembles the Classical Labyrinth shape. Cranes, like Storks, were feathered midwives.

It is recorded that, in certain French churches during the medieval period, choral dances were ritually performed in the labyrinth at Easter time. One such included the throwing of a ball between the Dean, who led the singing and his canons. Did the ball symbolise the Light of the World and was the dance to celebrate its rebirth?

To dance the labyrinth in a close chain with others, the dancers moving as one, produces a tremendous feeling of unity. There is a definite rhythm to the pattern of the labyrinth's pathways. No matter whether it is a classical seven or a Chartres eleven circuit, walk it regularly and you will soon begin to tune into its unique rhythm of clockwise/ anticlockwise, in an out, backwards and forwards. With familiarity, you will begin to relax into its pattern allowing yourself to surrender to its dynamic and to be danced by the pattern's strange attraction.

The pattern of the Classical Seven circuit labyrinth, for example takes us outwards for three circuits, to its perimeter. Then we loop back into circuit four, the central circuit and from thence we loop again in to the innermost seventh circuit, which is the first of three more outwards leading paths. Only then do we take the final loop into the centre.

Unknowingly we have traced a figure of eight, the mathematical symbol of infinity and the number of perpetual change, of death and rebirth. Unknowingly we have flipped over into a looking glass world and we flip back again on the outward journey.

Causing bodies to move or a rotor to revolve in a natural or magnetic field generates electricity. What power are we generating when we revolve around the centre of a labyrinth?

The pattern creates a potential whereby the positive and negative energies are brought into phase, neutralising each other, thereby creating a void space at the centre. A sacred vacuum.

Instructions for the Crane Dance

A line of dancers, their right thumb extended upwards and held by the left hand of the next dancer moves to the following rhythm, 1,2,3,4, pause ......

1. Place the Right foot ↙ behind the Left and rock backwards
2. Rock forwards onto the Left

Repeat 1 and 2

3. Close Right foot to left, touching the right toe lightly next to the left heel

Repeat 1 to 3 four times in all, whilst moving gradually to the right.

4. Step right →
5. Place left foot diagonally ↗ across it
6. Step right →
7. Take a small hop on the right foot, lifting the left knee
8. Place the left foot ↗ across the right

Repeat 4 to 8 four times in all

Meditation Five

A Pilgrimage

With its hidden symbolism of death and rebirth, and perhaps, its power to enable change, the labyrinth is an ideal place in which to atone for ones sins and find resolution of guilt or failure.

Prepare yourself to enter the labyrinth in the manner described earlier in the Alpha form.

Relax and sink your weight into the earth.
Breathe steadily, easily and deeply into the stomach.

Take one step, then another, and another.
Slowly, gently place one foot in front of another.
Feet well apart.
Weight evenly balanced.
Feel the weight shift, like sand running through an egg timer. Feel the weight shifting from one leg to another as you walk.
Feel the momentum of the movement carry you forward.

*Let your eyes focus gently on the unwinding path ahead.
Breathe easily and follow the path as gracefully as you can.
Let your arms hang at your sides – held out to the side a
little for balance.*

*Take the corners as smoothly as you can.
No stops and starts. No sudden shifts and jerks.
Gracefully.
Grace – when spirit inhabits body, when heaven meets
earth.*

*Allow your mind to focus on the deeds, thoughts or feelings
for which you feel guilt or of which you feel ashamed.
Do not attempt to justify or explain them.
Stay with the feelings of pain or discomfort as you walk.
Remembrance of failings past will come to mind.
Do not avoid them.
Allow the feelings of guilt to build.
Until you reach the centre.*

The place where there is nowhere else to go.

*Stop.
Stand still.
Motionless until the inner dynamic subsides.
Still centre within a turning world.*

*Feel the body's energy settle and sink deep into the earth
once more.*

Be aware once more of the four directions about you, heaven above and earth beneath.

Open yourself from your vulnerability to the possibility of forgiveness and redemption. Perhaps say a favourite prayer.

Ask and ye shall receive.

When the time is ripe, turn and retrace your steps. Imagine that you have left your guilt behind you in the vortex that is the centre of the labyrinth. Imagine that every step you take leads you closer to a position from which you can atone and make reparation.

Appropriate impulses of recompense and reconciliation may come to you on your outward journey. Remember them and act on them in the days and weeks to come.

When you reach the exit, turn and face the labyrinth.

Perform the closing practise as outlined earlier under Omega.

The Labyrinth & Pilgrimage

In the medieval Christian tradition it was believed that to traverse the labyrinth on ones knees was the equivalent to taking a pilgrimage to Jerusalem and pilgrims from all over Europe visited the labyrinths of the great Gothic cathedrals to perform this penance.

One of the finest ancient turf labyrinths in England can be found at Alkborough in South Humberside. Locals say that it was cut by the Benedictine monks who lived nearby between 1080 and 1220. It stands high on the northern escarpment of the Lincolnshire Wolds, overlooking the confluence of three rivers, the Humber, the Ouse and the Trent. Local myth has it that it was to this place that the four knights who murdered Thomas a Becket on the steps of the high altar of Canterbury Cathedral in 1170 came when they were ordered by the King to go to Jerusalem to seek penance.

The story has it that instead they high tailed it to the wilds of north Lincolnshire, lodged in "Jerusalem Cottage" in Alkborough village and made generous financial contributions to the building of the local church. And no doubt walked the labyrinth three times a day!

Whether the knights traversed the labyrinth on their knees or not, isn't known but it is interesting that the Knees are traditionally ruled by the zodiac sign of Capricorn, the sign governing the necessities, duties and responsibilities incurred through being incarnated in the physical world. In kneeling, we submit to the rules and limitations of life and surrender to higher forces. We bend the knee to that which has a greater authority.

The path of the labyrinth symbolises life's journey. We leave the familiar past behind and progress into an unknown future. We do not know where we are going but holding fast to faith, as Theseus held fast to Ariadne's thread, we are lead ever closer to the centre, to the sacred mystery of life.

The sacred value of the pilgrimage is recognised in all spiritual traditions. In choosing to undertake a journey to a Holy Place, we are released from the concerns of everyday life and are free to concentrate on spiritual concerns. During the journey we have time to reflect and to consider. We see meaning in events that we would normally be too preoccupied to notice. We are open to the magic of coincidence and synchronicity. We walk at our own pace.

No matter how wealthy or influential we are, no one can do it for us. We must do it for ourselves. No matter that the concerns of mundane reality must eventually reassert themselves, for this space of time we have chosen to devote ourselves to a spiritual goal and have our sights set on "higher things". And that experience stays with us, exerting a subtle and powerful influence on the rest of our lives, allowing us to see the mundane affairs of the physical plane from a different perspective. Every Muslim must undertake a pilgrimage to Mecca at some time in their life. It is interesting to note that their pilgrimage culminates in processing around the Ka'aba seven times, the same number of circuits as the classical and the Norwich Cathedral labyrinth! This practise is in fact a continuation of a pre-Islamic ritual which was meant to guarantee the maintenance of cosmic order, to guarantee that the Below proceeded in harmony with the Above.

The design of the Christian labyrinth superimposes a cross on the free flowing sweeps of the Classical pattern's multi-circuit structure. The cross is a universal symbol of great antiquity, long predating the life of Christ. It represents the four cardinal directions of space, north, south, east and west or the four elements of air, fire, earth and water, which are united at a fifth point, the sacred centre. The cross integrates these points into completion, oneness or wholeness at this central point.

In Christianity, the cross symbolises personal sacrifice and the suffering of crucifixion between polar opposites in order to transcend them. Interesting that Medieval icons commonly represented Christ crucified between paired opposites placed on opposing sides of the picture, for example, between the Sun and the Moon, between the good thief and the bad thief, between the lance and the chalice, between a man and a woman.

The pilgrim's journey through a Christian patterned labyrinth is therefore interrupted at those points where the path encounters an arm of the cross. The pilgrim is regularly turned back or impeded by forces beyond their control. In their journey, the pilgrim must traverse each quarter or part thereof in turn, between the arms of that cross, must enact the journey of their life within the constrictions imposed by the material world of the four elements and spatial directions.

We are all bound by limitation but the message of the labyrinthine pilgrimage is that in spite of this, the pathway still leads irrevocably to that central, sacred place of at-one-met, that place that is beyond polarity. The place where there is nowhere else to go.

Meditation Six

Contacting the Oracle

The form and energy of the labyrinth makes it a powerful pathway to reach that deep inner space within which the still, small voice of wisdom and inspiration can be heard. Even if that which "comes to you" does not make immediate sense, you will find that within the days that follow, dreams, coincidences or sudden realisations will bring a solution to your problem.

Prepare yourself to enter the labyrinth in the manner described earlier in the Alpha form.

Relax and sink your weight into the earth.
Breathe steadily, easily and deeply into the stomach.
Relax and sink your weight into the earth.
Breathe steadily, easily and deeply into the stomach.

Take one step, then another, and another.
Slowly, gently place one foot in front of another.
Feet well apart.
Weight evenly balanced.
Feel the weight shift, like sand running through an egg timer. Feel the weight shifting from one leg to another as you walk.

Feel the momentum of the movement carry you forward.

*Let your eyes focus gently on the unwinding path ahead.
Breathe easily and follow the path as gracefully as you can.
Let your arms hang at your sides – held out to the side a little for balance.*

*Take the corners as smoothly as you can.
No stops and starts. No sudden shifts and jerks.
Gracefully.
Grace – when spirit inhabits body, when heaven meets earth.*

*As you walk, focus on your question.
Try to keep not only the precise question in mind, but also hold within a questionning attitude.*

*A big question mark.
A request for help and guidance.*

Whenever you notice that your attention has wandered, bring your mind gently but firmly back to the question in mind.

*Let your feet walk its rhythm into the ground.
Let it inform the rhythm and pace of your walking.
Embody it. Repeat it over and over.
If it is an either/or question, focus on one option on the clockwise paths and on the other on the anticlockwise paths.*

Maintain your focus until you reach the centre.
Then stop and be still.
Still centre of a turning world

A touch to the forehead – think or say "as above".
Send your mind up into the sky as far as your imagination will carry you. Beyond the Moon. Out into the stars. See the solar system as if from outer space. Imagine hooking yourself into this spot.

A touch to the abdomen – think or say "so below".
Bring your mind down through your body into the earth beneath your feet. Imagine roots extending down into its centre, tapping into a hidden reservoir of magnetic fire.

A touch to the right shoulder – think or say " as before".
Project your mind to the far horizon and imagine the rest of your life stretching out before you into an unknown future.

A touch to the left shoulder – think or say "so behind".
Send your mind back into your past and be aware of the stream of events that has brought you to this time and place.

Prayer-like hands pointing upwards – think or say "as without".
Be aware of the four directions around you, their sounds, sights and smells.

Find a still, dark place deep within and rest there.

Prayer-like hands pointing down – think or say "so within"
Close your eyes for a moment and imagine energy from all around you flowing into your very centre.

Imagine that you are beyond Time,
Imagine that you are beyond Space.
Phrase your question once more, as clearly as you can.

And wait, with open mind.
Beathe deep into your body.
Relax.

See what comes to you.
What idea, or image first distracts you from that empty space?
This is your oracle.
Take note.
You may not understand it at first, but remember.

Now turn and retrace your steps.
Bear your answer in mind as you walk to the exit. Focus on it. Embody it, walk its words into your steps.

When you reach the exit, turn and face the labyrinth.

Perform the closing practise as outlined earlier under Omega.

MEDITATION SEVEN

Making Changes

The symbolism and power of the labyrinth makes it the perfect vehicle for personal rituals of rites of passage. Whether you are celebrating the change of season at the Solstice, getting married, scattering a loved one's ashes, giving up smoking or are on the threshold of any meaningful change in the pattern of your life, marking the occasion by walking the labyrinth will align you with the forces of change and ease the process of transition.

For sometime before your labyrinth walk, reflect upon the transition you are about to make. Select two objects.
 One that symbolises to you the energy of past times, of what you are leaving behind and another that represents everything you hope for from the new stage of life you are about to enter, the unknown future.
Place the object that symbolises the future in the centre of the labyrinth. You are allowed to go directly to the centre, across the lines, in order to do this.

Prepare yourself to enter the labyrinth in the manner described earlier in the Alpha form.

Holding the object that represents the past in your left hand, make a clear intent to leave all it represents behind you in the past.
Continue to hold it in your left hand as you
Relax and sink your weight into the earth.
Breathe steadily, easily and deeply into the stomach.

Take one step, then another, and another.
Slowly, gently place one foot in front of another.
Feet well apart.
Weight evenly balanced.
Feel the weight shift, like sand running through an egg timer. Feel the weight shifting from one leg to another as you walk.
Feel the momentum of the movement carry you forward.

Let your eyes focus gently on the unwinding path ahead.
Breathe easily and follow the path as gracefully as you can.
Let your arms hang at your sides – held out to the side a little for balance.

Take the corners as smoothly as you can.
No stops and starts. No sudden shifts and jerks.
Gracefully.
Grace – when spirit inhabits body, when heaven meets earth.

Look at the object in your hand as you walk and reflect upon the life path that has brought you to this threshold. Looking at the object in your hand, call to mind the people, places and events associated with those times. Observe them arising spontaneously from your memory and, without attachment, allow them to be superceded by other images.

Imagine them lying like so many leaves behind you on the path.
Imagine that you are shedding so many skins, so many attachments, so many things that have outlived their purpose and fruitfulness.

Leave it all behind you as you walk to the centre.
The place where there is nowhere else to go.
Stop.
Still centre of a turning world.
Keep your mind focussed on the past until no more images arise and the future beckons.

Feel the body's energy settle and sink deep into the earth.
Be aware once more of the four directions about you, of heaven above and earth beneath.

Feel your uniqueness. Hold the awareness that only you are here and now in this space and time.
Breathe deep into your body. Relax.
Then place the object you are carrying onto the earth and pick up that object you had placed there earlier, the one that speaks to you of your hopes for the future.

Hold it in your right hand as you make a wish or utter a prayer for this future.
Then turn and retrace your steps, holding it in both hands in front of you.

Keep your attention focussed on it as you walk slowly and steadily towards your new future.

Let your hopes for this time to come crystallise around it. Cultivate a wondering, expectant state of mind as you walk through the serpentine pathways from the opposite perspective.
Building a new foundation.

Ask for blessings and guidance.

When you reach the exit, turn and face the labyrinth. Transfer your symbolic object to your left hand and Perform the closing practise as outlined earlier under Omega.

Step out into the world renewed.
The future has begun.

Take the object home with you and put it somewhere where you will see it often and be reminded.

Labyrinth at NORWICH CATHEDRAL *designed by the author*